ZIP LINING THROUGH LIFE

TRAVELING THROUGH LIFE YAHUAH'S WAY

YAHNIECE

Publisher's Name: Yahniece

ISBN: 978-1-968442-75-0

ZIP LINING THROUGH LIFE

I recommend Zip Lining to anyone who is controlling, fearful, afraid of heights, doubtful, double-minded, full of anxiety, stressed, or depressed. Truth be told, I was quite a few of these things. Okay, okay, all of these things. And zip lining showed me how I needed to overcome all of those areas with the Ruach HaKodesh's (Yahuah's Spirit) help, because you can't do anything in His will without Him. It was crazy and amazing to me how I learned a lot spiritually about myself on this adventure. And I can't wait to tell you how, but first, let me give you a little background on me.

I was (before complete surrender and obedience) to Yahuah what most would call a controlling, headstrong, "I can't count on anybody but myself" type of person. I love Yahuah with all that is within me, but boy, did I have emotional baggage and didn't even realize it. Yahuah has been so patient with me, teaching me patience —for myself and others. Praise Yahuah that I am a work in progress until Yahusha returns (Philippians 1:6), and I am so happy that He has not given up on me and my shenanigans. I have truly been a handful, and that is why I adore Yah so much. Just so we are clear, I call our creator 'Yahuah' —ABBA — because He truly is my father, so you will notice me saying that throughout my story.

Yahusha knew that leaving His Ruach HaKodesh here when He ascended to heaven was necessary, especially for me (John 14:15–31), to dwell inside me and get me right-minded. I am blessed with the amazing opportunity to publish this precious little book twice, as it has been updated based on my journey from this experience in 2015. And where I am now in 2025 (completely out of my forest season), healed, delivered, and set free from the bondage of the enemy. I was truly a captive because of all the idols I carried.

Extreme traumas from childhood through adulthood that demons used to feed on and keep me bound and captive. I am now who Yahuah created me to be. I, along with my heavenly Father, love me some me! For the first time in my life, I am getting to know our Creator, and in Him, I am learning who I am and who He created me to be. I am now a servant for the Most High, focused on setting the Chosen captives free (Dry bones/Remnants) for as long as I am here on this earth. Not only that, but my job is also to teach them how to have a real relationship with our creator, make sure they are filled with His Ruach, and walking in obedience. How I'm able to help people is because I've experienced it myself. It's my testimony.

So, before I continue, I want to speak on something I learned towards the end of my forest season. And if you don't understand "Forest Season", let me briefly explain that as well. My ancestors that are spoken about in the Bible, whom Abba calls a stiff-necked people (Exodus 32:9; Acts 7:51), Yes, Abba also taught me that my ancestors are the original Israelites. Blew me away! They were in the forest for 40 years. And spiritually, once we allow His Ruach HaKodesh to fill us, there is a process that we have to go through to be healed, delivered, and set free, which includes fasting, and spiritually we have our own personal forest season. how long you're in that season depends on you and your obedience to Yahuah. And how quickly we are able to give up our idols. Abba taught me that we must all commit to a 40-day fast, and that fast is between you and Him. Just like Daniel had his own fast, Yahuah gives us our own fast. You simply must ask Him how He wants you to fast. Simply put, fasting is NO FOOD!

There can be different levels based on your situation, but again, that is between you and Yahuah. At that point, we are letting Yahuah know that we have surrendered all and that it is time for Him to start showing us the idols that we carry, so that we can surrender them to Him for healing and deliverance. I remember just wishing I would wake up one day and be healed, delivered, and set free. But it doesn't work that way: Yahuah doesn't work that way. And He deals with all His children the same way (Hebrews 13:8). And baby, let me tell you, it is a process, and it can be a long one if you're not completely obedient. Obedience is key to getting out of your forest season. And most importantly, it is how you show Yahuah you love Him. (John 10:27) Yahuah taught me what I must do in order to get through the forest as quickly and painlessly as possible.

Here are the five things:

1. Pray without ceasing—talk to and listen for Abba all day, every day. Imagine you are climbing into your father's lap, snuggling up to him and telling Him everything that is on your heart. He already knows anyway, so you might as well get comfortable sharing with Yahuah how you truly feel about everything. Abiding (sitting for more than 5 minutes listening for Yahuah to respond) is an important part of your relationship. It's not just about talking to Abba and telling Him your needs; it's mostly about sitting and just being with Him and listening for Him. He speaks to you in many different ways.

   A.From His spirit (Ruach ha Kodesh) to your spirit.
   B. Through reading your Bible.
   C. Or through others, like watching a prophet on TikTok.

   He will reach you when and how He sees fit. This is how you learn how to be a daughter/son of the Most High Elohym. You will know because you will feel a quickening in your spirit, which means you will just know it's Him and it's truth, and the truth will set you free. You just have to receive what He has to say and obey immediately.

2. Read your Bible—Like your life depends on it, because it does. Abba wants you to read it like it's the love story that it truly is from Yahuah, from beginning to end, straight through. No matter how long it takes, and don't skip around. It is food for your soul, and when you get to Revelation, start over. The Torah (Old Testament) is how you get to know Yahuah (Our creator). You will get to know Him when He is loving, when He is angry, and even when He is sad and hurting. You will get to know how He deals with, protects, and disciplines His children. It is essential to your life to read this book that Yahuah has sustained all these centuries for you to hear from Him. People are walking around today, and their souls are starving to death, because it has never been fed properly. Instead, they are trying to feed their souls with pagan things, which gives only a temporary happiness. And sadly, people spend way too much time and money on their flesh, which will just go right back to dust when they die. It's your soul that you should be paying attention to and taking care of. And trust me, I know sometimes reading the Bible can be so confusing. But that is where His Spirit (Ruach ha Kodesh) comes in to give you clarity. Even if you don't understand some parts, it is still feeding your soul and giving you strength spiritually. Keep reading! And get the missing books that were taken out by the Catholics. They are all anointed by Yahuah.—the Bible is alive! It's Yahuah's word, you can read the same scripture multiple times and get a different meaning each time because once you have asked Him to fill you with His Spirit, it unlocks the secrets that Yahuah has placed there just for you.

3. Fasting—needs to become a part of your life. All five of these are essential for your life and relationship with Yahuah. I started fasting one day a week because I like to remind Yahuah and myself (because I am a foodie, let's be honest) that I love Him more than food. Fasting allows you to die to self, and as your body is submitting, you are submitting to Yahuah. Fasting to die to your flesh actually allows you to hear Him better. Yes, trust me, I know it's hard. Nobody likes to be hungry. But here's some great information: Yahuah created our bodies to be able to heal itself. But it will only do it when you fast. He is truly amazing. So again, yes, trust me I know it's hard, but it is so worth it.

4. Worship—This is how you fight the enemy and get prayers answered with your WARship. Do it every day, all day if you can. When I walk my doggies, I put my worship music on and I just sing my heart out to my Elohim. He loves it. He says it's like a sweet aroma (Psalms 141:2). And demons hate it—they run from it. It's warfare, and it calls on Yah's angels to fight for you. And last but not least:

5. Abstain—If you are single, you need to abstain from all lust and fornication because Abba created sex for marriage, PERIOD. Anything outside of that, you are cursing your own body (1 Corinthians 6:18). Also, abstain from anything that you put before Yahuah (First Commandment). Whether that is alcohol, drugs, overeating, or eating unhealthily, your body is a temple that houses Yahuah's Ruach HaKodesh. You must take care of your temple. You only get one body (Vessel). And you must guard your eye gates, ear gates, and anything that you receive in your body. What that means is pay attention to and discern what you are watching and listening to and eating. This isn't going to be easy, you're going to have to

surrender it to Elohim. Now keep in mind that you will not be able to do any of these things without Yahuah's Spirit helping you. So, you must learn how to ask Yahuah to help you and surrender things to Him daily. So that He will indeed help you. And trust me, He will when He sees that you're serious about surrendering and having a real relationship with Him. He will start showing you things that you didn't even know you carried. Ask me how I know…Because I had to learn this the hard way, you can't do anything without Yahuah in the name of His son YAHUSHA.

Okay, I think I made the forest reference clear. Now I want to speak on our Creator's name. When I finally got serious and told our heavenly Father that I wanted to know Him, I wanted to know everything about Him. I was singing it one day to Him, and He responded to me. He said, clear as day, "Start with my name." I asked Him "What do you mean, Father?" Your name is God and Lord and Jesus, right?" Boy, was I wrong. Abba speaks to me through YouTube and any other way that He can get my attention, which is amazing. I believe within that hour, I turned my television on, and a video popped up speaking about our creator's name. The first thing I learned is that the Greeks and Romans took His name out of the Bible over 6000 times! "God" means a pagan god named Baal, and "Lord" is just a title, It's not a real name. Our creator has a name (Isaiah 42:8). And in doing further research, I found out His name. His name is Yahuah. These new Jews changed it stating that we are not worthy of ever saying His name, which is a lie. The Bible speaks about His name many times and how great His name is. Before His real name was taken out of the bible it was there 6200+ times. And His Son, who came and died for us, said "I came in my father's name." (John 5:43) Which is Yahusha, which means Yah saves. That is why we sing HalleluYAH. I couldn't believe I had been singing that hymn all my life, not realizing His real name is in it.

Our creator chose Hebrew people to be His chosen priests in this sinful world. Israel is a people, not a place. His son, who came and died for us was a Hebrew man with a Hebrew name. And man had the audacity to change His name—not translated or even transliterate it. They completely changed His name! Which I now know was Mastema (Satan), demons have worked to deceive us for centuries. Because His name is so powerful. Satan was on a crusade to trick, deceive, and lie to everyone, starting with the Creator's real name. Yahuah said that He will help deceive the world in these last days (2 Thessalonians 2:11-12) Because He only wants the people that truly are seeking Him with their whole heart. If you are truly seeking to have a real relationship with our creator the most high Yahuah, He will show up —guaranteed. Don't take my word for it; do your own research. He said if you seek him, you will find him (Jeremiah 29:13). And that is exactly what I was doing. And in doing that, my life changed forever.

He was teaching me and is still teaching me so much. My mind is blown with all the things He has shared with me. He is showing me secrets that have had my mouth hanging open for weeks! The biggest one was realizing that my ancestors are the people in the Bible! That the people that are on the land they call Israel are counterfeits! And that the promised land isn't where they say Israel is. Mastema (satan) has been hiding our identity from us for centuries. For those that have never heard his name, Mastema can be found in the Book of Jubilees: This is the main source for information on Mastema. In this book, Mastema is the angel who rules over a tenth of the evil spirits (Nephilim), after the Flood. He is portrayed as an adversary who tests humanity's faith and carries out divine punishments.

Choosing to live righteously and set apart "Qodeshim"

Becoming who Yahuah created you to be is a strenuous process that you have to go through with Yah's Ruach HaKodesh's guidance and help. When you decide to live your life for Yahuah and sincerely commit to it, what you need to realize is that, in order for Yahuah to be able to live inside of you and use you for His glory, there has to be some serious house cleaning in your heart (Deliverance)(2 Corinthians 5:17).

What I didn't realize was that I had a ton of baggage that Abba had to:

1. Reveal to me.
2. Then I had to acknowledge it and realize where they came from (e.g. childhood traumas, military traumas, etc).
3. Repent for being an emotional hoarder, and
4. Ask Yahuah to heal, deliver, set me free, and create in me a clean heart (Psalms 51:10).

Boy, I did not know what a challenge that was going to be. Paul said, "I die daily" (1 Corinthians 15:31). That means giving up your own will and fleshly desires and choosing ABBA's will for your life. (die to self). I have learned in my research the Israelites in the Bible were my ancestors. So, it's no surprise that I am just like them—always begging Yahuah to get us out of bondage (Debt, bad relationships, bad jobs, sickness, etc). Promising Him if He does we will live for Him (lies). And because of our selfish, fleshly ways, or as Yahuah put it "we are a stiff-necked people (Exodus 32:9)". That's why it took them 40 years to go on a 40 day journey. And the same applies to us: it will be a journey to our destiny that Yahuah has planned for us. (Jeremiah 29:11) Elohim has to prepare us for what He has in store for our destiny. In getting to know Yahuah, we will learn who He created us to be. And He will not bless us with it until He knows we are ready. He learned from our ancestors that giving them what they wanted first (the exodus from Egypt) led to Him doing His part, and we as a nation breaking our part of the covenant. This is why we are cursed as a people (Deuteronomy 28). Our problem is that we don't like to wait on Him, so we try to do things our own way—which is not smart because we don't know the future; He does.

Looking back at the start of my journey till now.

As I updated this anointed little book, I sat back and pondered where I was spiritually when I first published this book back in 2015. I'm absolutely amazed at all the things that I have been through on this 10-year journey. I am going to attempt to describe how it feels spiritually to enter the forest. It must have been amazing for my ancestors exiting Egypt, leaving their homes where they were able to cook food and sleep in their beds. I would guess it had to be more comfortable than lying on the ground in the forest. I can imagine the culture shock of entering the wilderness for the first time and what they had to deal with. For me, entering my seasons felt like I was in quicksand, and Yahuah was holding my head up so I could breathe until I came to a place of submission. I had to come to the realization that I needed Yahuah to be in charge of my life, to take the wheel, as people say. Once you repent, give your life to our Heavenly Father, and ask Him to fill you with His Spirit, He becomes relentless. He promises to never leave, nor forsake us —He will not fail (Hebrews 13:5). His goal is to create in you a clean heart, so that you can become everything He created you to be. So, you better hold on, receive His peace, and use that gift of joy that gives you strength and never let go. You are in for a bumpy ride, but well worth it in the end. Your life will be changed, let me correct that YOU will be changed forever. Because the change begins in you and flows out. So that you can help others learn the truth of salvation, and healing.

Looking back at all the things that I went through from then until now, It makes complete sense as to why Abba says now is the time to share my book. One of the things I've learned about myself that has changed, thanks to Yahuah, is when He would tell me things. I would take that idea or that vision and run with it. Until I realized I was running by myself, and I had to go back to where Abba told me about the vision and allow Him to lead. Well, that's what happened with this book, and that's why it didn't go anywhere when I published it the first time. The publishing company literally folded right after they printed my little book. I think I probably sold five copies, and that was at my book signing. It truly makes sense now, coming out of my forest season, to write everything down and share it with those who have yet to experience it or to those who are actually going through it and need a little encouragement. It would've been great to have that while I was going through it myself. I have never met anyone who was a true obedient faith walker. I have never been able to have someone help me understand this crazy and amazing journey. The biggest part while Yahuah is dealing with you is the enemy fighting you hardcore the entire time. He doesn't want you to know who you are. He doesn't want you to become who Yahuah created you to be. Because once you realize who you are, you become a threat to his evil kingdom. It has been just Yahuah and me for 4 years straight (2021-2025), and I preferred it that way. I was just telling my journal how I would beg and plead with Abba, saying that I want to be as close to Him as Moses was, as Abraham, Isaac and Jacob were. And I'm learning to be closer to Him more and more each day. Everyone else has to go away. It has to literally be just myself and His Ruach (Spirit), because there are things that He will share with me that no one else needs to know. They wouldn't understand anyway. No one understands your journey, but you and Yahuah.

Isolation is a real thing. I have to remember that the enemy doesn't create anything. He just copies, counterfeits, and perverts. When people go into isolation, where the enemy tries to keep you from everybody so that he can torment you and convince you to kill yourself. I should have known that isolation comes from Yahuah for good reasons, and Satan took it and made it bad. Because the isolation that I have been in for the past four years has been extreme, yet very necessary. Yahuah had to get rid of all the people that can't go with me into my harvest season and my destiny. That was truly hard for me because I didn't know who I was, and I always felt like I had to have people around me to tell me. I remember when I couldn't make a decision without talking to my ex-best friend or my ex-father about everything. It was terrible. I had no confidence in myself whatsoever. And truly, the only one that can show me who I am and lead me in this life is Yahuah. Yahuah had to teach that, by getting me alone with just Him so that I would learn how to hear His voice whenever He spoke to me. So if I can help anyone understand the molding, shaping, and pruning process that you must go through in the forest, I'm here to help. I plan to write another book about my life, because I know I am not the only one that has gone through all the crazy things that I have gone through in my lifetime. And I'm hoping to share my story to help encourage and educate someone else.

A ton of lessons I had to learn

I have learned that when we are born, we are blessed with gifts to use for the Most High's glory ONLY. I know some of you will say, "But I want to do what I want with my life". Well, I'm sorry—you didn't create yourself so you don't have that right. But you do have the will to choose who you will serve for all eternity. He is a gentleman and only wants the people that choose Him and love Him sincerely. Sadly, most people use their gifts for their own gratification and recognition, when in most cases, they had nothing to do with it. It's all by His grace. All things good come from Yahuah (James 1:17). On judgment day, we will all have to give an account for the gifts and the life that He has given us. One of my gifts from Abba is that I am a worshipper, and I have an anointing on my voice. I am a prophetic warrior for the Most High. Yahuah uses me to speak to His chosen people who are in bondage and sadly don't even realize it in most cases.

I realized just this past year that I lost my voice when I was a little girl. Mastema (Satan) figured out a way to take it from me, and he didn't hesitate. I believe Mastema knows who the chosen ones are from birth and he and his evil spirits start to attack us as children and continues to attack all of our lives to keep us from having a real relationship with Yahuah. I realized I lost my voice because I was always afraid to tell anybody what I was experiencing (child abuse and molestation) or if I wasn't satisfied or happy.

I remember exactly when it happened. I was being molested by my cousins on my father's side of the family. On one horrible occasion, my dad actually caught the boys and punished me for it! And he never spoke to me about what happened. He just made me stand in the corner when we got home for an hour. So, at that moment, I told myself I would never say anything because nobody would listen. I never spoke about the abuse I experienced as a child to anyone. And looking back, I was really abused, by my mother, my cousins, and at my daycare. The enemy was after me from the start. So, it makes sense to me now why I was always afraid to speak up about anything. I was even afraid to sing. I never thought anyone would care to listen. But Yahuah gave me my voice back in 2024, and then I had to learn how to tweak it because I was just telling everybody off about everything lol, the truth can sting. I mean before I got my voice back, it was terrible. If someone did my hair badly, I would tip them and never say anything. I was emotionally abused by my ex-husband for nine years and barely complained about any of it. I think I felt I deserved it. So, as you can see, I had a lot of baggage that Yahuah had to sift through and clean out of me starting with showing me love, showing me what real love is. For He is love. So if you have not experienced Yahuah's love, you don't know what REAL love is…

Yahuah will not give you more than you can handle.

Well, I used to argue with Yahuah quite a bit about this (actually argue with myself because Yah doesn't argue since He's always right). I would stumble over a spiritual obstacle the enemy set up for me and say, "Really, Really Holy Spirit!!! I seriously doubt if I can handle this!" I used to say Holy Spirit because that is what I was taught in Christianity to say. That's actually a pagan name (more info on this in the glossary). So, I don't use it anymore, I found out it's actually Yahuah's spirit which is Ruach HaKodesh or simply His Ruach (spirit). I stepped away from Christianity years ago when I realized it's a religion that leads you astray just like all the others. It's a trap from the enemy. They are not following Yahuah's covenants and laws. They separate us from the Hebrews in the Bible. And make us believe we are the gentiles "Christians" If you read the Bible for yourself from beginning to end, you will see the truth for yourself. I digress back to what I was saying—and then I would try on my own and fail miserably (Holy Ghost Jr.- it's what my auntie Penny used to call me)

When I lost my spiritual Mother and my brother within three weeks of each other to start my 2013 off (she passed on New Year's Day, and my brother passed 3 weeks later), I just knew Yahuah made a mistake in thinking I could handle that. My aunt, who was my spiritual mother and whom I lovingly called my binky (security blanket), When I couldn't hear from Yahuah (because I was too busy being Holy ghost Jr.) I would call Auntie Penny, and Yahuah would speak through her to me) When I was hurting beyond repair, I would call my auntie, and she would always listen to me rant and cry. And when I would stop to take a breath or to hear what Yahuah had put on her heart to say. There would be a long silent pause. I would panic and say, "Auntie, are you still there!" thinking I lost my signal and would have to call back and start all over again with my pity party. She would always tell me that she was listening to the Holy Spirit (Ruach). And then Yahuah would give me a spiritual spanking I really needed, mostly for my unbelief and doubt, or a gentle reminder that He loves me so much, that I am on the right path, and I need to let Him handle my battles. But the last time I spoke with my sweet and loving auntie, Yahuah told me to study His word like never before. He kept saying over and over, "My word, My word Niecey, study My word". I think He was preparing me for what was to come. Yahuah was preparing me to lose my binky (my auntie Penny) here on earth.

I would have to clear my mind of all the mess, so I could hear Him for myself. And being in His word was the sure way to do that. You see, clearing my mind is my job, and renewing my heart is Yahuah's job. Yahuah had to send me some of His medicine He created to help me with my mind. Trauma tends to stay with you all your life until the Most High delivers you. And because of trauma, you can't be your true self. I will tell you all about how Hemp (cannabis herb from Yahuah) saved my mind in another book. What I will tell you is Yahuah put everything growing out of this earth that we need to stay healthy and healed. But we as humanity choose man-made drugs instead, which never fix the issue. It just puts a Band-Aid on it so that they can keep us sick for money/profits. And if you don't know who they are, you need to pray more. Now back to my story.

I felt like Yahuah literally held me up that entire day. Every time I would think about my Auntie and how I was going to face even one day without her, my knees would start to buckle. I literally had five flights to work that day with a smile on my face. Yahuah kept reminding me that she is with Him, and there is no place better than that. Talk about having mixed feelings. I wanted to be happy for her, but what about me? I wanted to scream! Yep, I too can be selfish. When I finally got to my hotel room, I laid on the floor and wept deeply from my soul for hours. I cried for all the times I wanted to call her but didn't because I didn't want to bother her. I wept for all the years I avoided her because I was living in sin and thought she could see all my dirt. I told Yahuah I needed a hug, like my auntie used to tell me she would get.from Him when she needed it.

If you have never felt a hug from Yahuah, you are missing something amazing. There is a peace that comes over you and a joy that makes no sense to the mind, but the heart just melts. And every time I think about my Binky now, I know that she is in the presence of the Most High. She is standing in the gap for me and cheering me on. (I'm not sure if that is biblically correct, but it's my happy place).

My brother leaving us was painful in a sad and peaceful sort of way. Yahuah told me a couple of years prior to his death that He would save the one that pulled deeply on my heart, and that was my brother Boo (that's what we called him). He was very sick and always struggled in every aspect of his life. It was crazy because three months before he passed, his heart stopped, and it took 20 minutes for the paramedics to bring him back. And what that did was allow him to spend time with his kids, and mend broken hearts, and also allowed him to mend his relationship with my father, who led him to Yahuah

Three months after his first heart attack, he had another one, and no one was around to help him. Yahuah saved him by taking him from all of his pain and suffering. Some of us don't finish the race, but because of Yahuah's grace, we still make it into His rest. I dealt with a lot of guilt about my brother because I wasn't a good sister to him. He was always that annoying little brother who wanted nothing but to be with me all the time. I had to ask Abba to forgive me, and I had to forgive myself. But I loved him dearly and will miss him calling me Niecebutt (no amount of boxing his ears, would stop him from calling me that smh) But I am so happy that I will see him again with my mother, my auntie, and so many other people I love who knew Yahusha. So, I was dealing with that and the fact that life was kicking me in my behind as per usual. The enemy of my soul was trying to destroy me, and I didn't even know it! You see most chosen ones don't realize that we are at war spiritually. The enemy of our soul waged war on us through Adam and he takes it very seriously. Unfortunately, most of us don't. That is Mastema's advantage, the fact that we don't take him seriously. So, I was an emotional wreck. I couldn't stop crying. I can't even put into words how I felt. My heart just hurt. I was in a marriage that was literally killing me softly, and I just wanted to end it all…

Until I experienced zip lining! It could not have come at a more perfect time. I was about to give up on life! I had been through so much in my life. My self-esteem had been crushed, my heart had been broken, I had nothing left in me. I asked Yahuah to please help me breathe. I couldn't breathe… My amazing friend Brandi, whom I know Yahuah put in my life, told me that she wanted me to go Ziplining with her and some other girlfriends for her birthday. My first thought was, heck no! I don't do stuff like that! But something pulled at my shattered heart to go. I always have such a wonderful time when I get to hang with her, and it's not often enough. And when we do get to hang out, it's usually doing something bad like eating desserts, we have no business eating.

And you can't tell Brande no; she can be very convincing. So, I decided to go. I needed to have some fun and get my joy back.

What was I thinking! I never gave much thought about what Zip lining was exactly. I think if I had really researched what Zip lining was, I would not have gone. As a matter of fact, I know I would not have gone! Yahuah would have to come down here Himself and tell me to do that again, and I would still have a tantrum. And Abba knew that.... This was truly a spiritual experience for me that Yahuah had His hand in. This was the introduction to my forest season spiritually.

Everything I have been going through my entire life with ABBA's Ruach ha Kodesh was completely right before my eyes above the trees (did I mention I'm afraid of heights?) with huge carpenter bees flying around us (they live up there) on a very small platform we were on that sways with the wind and vibrates whenever someone zips. There were eight of us plus the guide on this little platform above the trees. Can you picture this now?!? I never felt more helpless and completely out of control in my life! (Yes, I am controlling—well I used to be [*sigh*]) It just showed me my life and what I have been going through and just how much I really trust my creator or don't trust Him is more like it. Once I committed to zip lining (living my life as Yahusha did in exchange for Him dying for me), I realized that phrase I have been telling myself and other people was all wrong! It is actually Yahuah will always give you more than you can handle, because He wants you to realize you can't do anything without Him! I had to learn to let go and allow Yahuah to lead me in every aspect of my life. I mean everything he wants to be involved in everything.

Ok let's get back to my zip lining experience…I had to climb a really high ladder to a platform, that was four stories high and zipped my very first zip line (terrified). It sounds pretty simple, but it took my guide about 20 minutes to pry my fingers from around the tree (yes, I quickly became a tree hugger), we were on and get me latched on the line. But that was not the worst part. I did not realize it was the smallest and shortest one of all six zips I had to do to finally be finished (a small detail my mischievous friend Brandi forgot to tell me!) Yes, I said six, and yes, I said the only way to get down once you did your first zip (it zipped higher each time) was to zip line to the next platform that was smaller!!! I just knew I was going to have a heart attack! I kept explaining (yelling hysterically) to my guide that I could not do this! That I was not strong enough! And he kept very patiently telling me, yes, I can because he's got me and he won't ever let me fall. He kept showing me on each platform the harnesses and the heavy-duty clamps that are in place to protect me. Then he told me, "But the only thing I can't help you overcome is your fear". I yelled at him with tears in my eyes and said "yes you can! You can do anything! I was literally speaking to Yah and didn't realize it at the time. At this very moment, even though I could visually see that I was safely strapped to the line with huge hooks that could not break under my weight, my mind kept screaming "I'm gonna die!" I allowed reasoning to overcome my faith. We do that a lot as believers! Yahuah will tell us in our spirit to do something, and we will allow our minds (reasoning) to talk us out of it. Sometimes we just need to step out in faith and trust what Ruach is telling us. Then go with me!" I cried, and he said "I can't, but I believe in you and I know you can do it". "How do you know that!" I whined hysterically and every time he would move his hand off me so I could go I would freak out! "Don't let me go!" I yelled at the top of my lungs. And he would put his hand back and say "I am here" each time with my entire body shaking and with me screaming at the top of my lungs, "Jesus" (this was before I knew His real name is Yahusha) until I made it to the other side. I could only look back for a second so as to never forget what I accomplished with Abba's help. And feel so peaceful, healed, and so full of love for Yahuah I thought my chest would burst. Then I would take a moment and enjoy the beauty of His creation and the company of my friends, who are going through this with me overcoming their own fears in their own way. Only to realize—it ain't over! There is more, and it's worse than before! Did I mention there were huge bees! Not only was I afraid of heights, but I was also terrified of bees. My brother (Boo) and I fell on a beehive when we were little. Let me tell you that crazy story.

My cousin was throwing the football to us in our backyard. And unbeknownst to us, a beehive had fallen from the telephone pole above our yard into the tall grass. I went running backwards trying to catch the football, and fell exactly where the hive was (I caught the football, by the way) When I felt the first couple of stings, I was about to get up when my brother fell on top of me. By the time I got him off me, bees were all in my clothes, my hair, and mouth because I was screaming so loud. He got stung once and took off running toward the house, with me running behind him. My cousin saw the bees and ran into the house ahead of us. My mother was in the house cleaning and worshipping, like always, and heard all the screams. When she saw us with a million bees over our heads stinging and chasing us into the house from the back door, like a cartoon. She screamed and ran out the front door. So, we were chasing my mom down the street to get the bees off us, and she was running down the street screaming, trying to get away from the bees. It was a hilarious sight to see, although it wasn't funny to us at the time. Our neighbors had to stop my mother and help shoo the bees away.

Once everything calmed down, we counted 32 bee stings on my puny little body, and about five on my brother's. My neighbors thought that was the funniest scene they had ever witnessed. I, however, could not find the humor in it until I tell the story now. The people on my block laughed about that for weeks. So, on the zip line platform, when I saw those bees (which were the size of quarters) I almost fainted. You can't run or swat at them because there are nine of you above the trees on a platform the size of a bath towel! Spiritually, I saw those bees as demons in my life. Yahuah doesn't want us spending time fighting with demons. (2 Chronicles 20:15) He wants us to ignore them and stay focused on Him and trust Him completely during the time in the forest. And worship with all our hearts. Because worship is the water that drowns our enemy. And I did just that because I had no choice! Trying to swat the bees would've made my stress level even worse.

You see, once you sincerely commit your life to Yahuah, He will not let you go or let you quit, (Matt 18:12-14; Luke 15:3-7). Yahuah will never give up on you… (This picture is of me and Brandi, who was doing the zips like she's been doing them all her life—smh, I was crawling up the stairs. I was so terrified.)

But a lot of times (sadly), we give up on ourselves, not realizing that the process Yah is allowing us to go through is to strengthen us and help us walk someone else through what we have been through. Nothing is wasted. (Romans 8:28-30) When I look backnow, here in 2026 at that experience, I am so different. Now I have more courage. I'm bolder because I know who I am, and I know that my creator loves me and that He takes very good care of me. So, my confidence level is amazing. I just might try zip lining again. I can't believe I'm saying that!

My guide kept telling me to take all the time I needed, but he said, "I'm going to the next platform (season)". At one point, I had to look at him and make sure Yahusha wasn't standing there right next to me

(John 21:4). Every time I would let go and just allow my harness to carry me (at neck-breaking speed) to the next platform and I would take a second to stop screaming and breathe I felt peace and joy. Ok, so five down, one more platform to go and I am out of this forest (did I mention I wasn't really a nature person either—sheesh). We are finally on the ground, and I am saying to myself, "Thank you, Jesus!" (Again this is before I learned His real name). Then I said really loud to my guide and friends, "I am done, you should have never let me touch the ground! I am not going on another platform!" And I meant it!

It's amazing what the right amount of peer pressure and encouragement can do for a person. But I went kicking and screaming! I did not want to experience that again! Brandi had to give her mom Xanax to get her to finish, we were planning an escape lol. So, I told myself that I will walk with them to the next platform, and then I would make a run for it.

It was a beautiful walk past a lake and a graveyard! GRAVEYARD!!! What the?! Really?! Really! I yelled "it's time to go", I am done! I can't take no more! I have accomplished everything I need to accomplish! I am good! I tell them. My guide just laughs and keeps on walking ahead. Because what he knew that I didn't realize yet was that I was completely lost! Even if I took off running in the other direction, I didn't know how to get out of the forest without him. And he was going to the next platform that was the highest, the longest, the scariest, and the way out of the forest! Now there was a sweet older lady with us who was going through this entire experience crying and fussing like me—Brandi's mom. I was so irritated with her, though, because she didn't give up! And there was no way I was going to quit before her! So, I just knew when we arrived at that last platform she was going to say "heck no!" And I would be free!! Well she did say heck no and a few other things I better not repeat. But our guide and our peers would not let her quit. They took her hands and helped her slowly walk (excuse me) climb up about one hundred spiraling steps around an oak tree that kept swaying with each step! I wanted to cry; I was so frustrated at this point. My guide would not even respond to my tantrum at the bottom, on the ground where I felt safe. When they all got halfway up, he looked over the spiral stairs down at me and said "Come on, V, you can do it!" I think I called him a name at this point and yelled "You don't know me! I'm telling you I can't and I won't!" (Jeremiah 1:5)

They climbed a few more steps, and I am thinking to myself, I don't even have a good sense of direction! I have come so far with this crazy guide that I can't do anything without him! And I realized—I don't want to! And that is where Yahuah has me right now in my life. He has gotten me so far with His grace and mercy, and I know I have more ahead of me (Romans 8:36-39). But I cannot do it without Him nor do I want to. And I am so deeply in love with Him. I can't quit, I won't quit. I realize that He didn't put that in me. I don't know how to quit. I don't know what that looks like, so I push forward because I know Yahuah has me.

Escape the forest on my own

So, I decided to make a run for it anyway and take my chances on the ground where I felt safe and in control. And right when I was about to take a step, my guide yelled down at me from the top of the platform, "Don't make me come down and get you! And I will be pissed when I get there if you make me do this three times!" (Climbing those steep stairs could not have been easy) I was so shocked that he knew what I was going to attempt! And even more shocked, that he yelled and threatened me! So, I decided I was going to go up there and give him a piece of my mind. Who does he think he's talking to! And then I was going to walk right back down those steps. Well, as I was grumbling on my way up by myself (Hugging a tree and climbing it is quite challenging), I really didn't realize how high it was. By the time I was halfway up, I nearly fainted when I tried to look down. I was too scared to go back down from the halfway point! What a pickle I was in! "This is some Bull" I yelled "Black people don't do crazy stuff like this!" I yelled. Right when I said that, I looked down to see a whole group of probably my cousins heading to their next line with their guide! Looking just as happy and excited. Don't you hate it when you are going through things, and you want someone to pity you instead of praying for you? And they are so happy to tell you to hang in there, the Most High has you. Or just trust Abba, He loves you. Even though it's the last thing we feel we want to hear right then, it's what we need to hear. So, I kept climbing....

When I finally made it to the top, on my hands and knees (there was no way I could stand up), I wish I could explain to you how I felt at that very moment. All thoughts of strangling my guide went out the window. I needed him so badly right then. Off went the last person to the other side of the forest, and it was just me and the guide. My eyes filled up with tears.

He took my hands and helped me stand up. My entire body was shaking. And when I looked into his eyes, all I saw was pride and admiration for what I had accomplished. He told me he didn't think I would finish this course. He honestly thought I would have given up after the first line. He told me I overcame my fear, and I will do it again. At that moment, I realized my legs weren't shaking as much as they were before. And I also realized that, as he was speaking to me, he was hooking me to the line and I was ready to go. But he didn't push me. Not once did he ever force me to go. Each time, he allowed me to let go when I was ready. And the last thing I said to him before I let go was "I'm going to make you proud this time," and I let go.

This time, it was so long that after screaming as long as I could, I stopped to take a breath and take in the beauty of what was around me. I went over the lake we had walked past; it was gorgeous! The wind was blowing so sweetly, and the sky was so clear and beautiful. And then, about 20 feet away from the last platform I will ever have to stand on, the wind stopped me from moving! "Noooooo!" I yelled with sheer frustration and fear. I was over the lake, and I couldn't swim! I was stuck and had no idea how to get to the platform.

Just when I was about to start crying, I could hear my friends yelling for me to flip over and use my arms to pull myself to the platform. What?! Seriously?! Abba, can't any of this be easy! So, I flipped myself over and started pulling myself upside down towards the final platform. I told myself I was going to strangle my guide when I got there. That was my motivation to do it. And I did it! With adrenaline pumping and thoughts of beating my guide to death when I'm finally on the ground keeping me motivated. I was so close and so tired! My arms couldn't pull me another inch. I kept yelling for my guide to come out and get me, and he kept saying "I'm coming keep pulling!" He had no intentions of coming out there, by the way. Before I knew it, I had pulled myself all the way to the platform and was done. My guide was grinning from ear to ear. I told him if my arms weren't so sore, I would strangle him. But I seriously could not lift one finger. I did it!! I made it through the forest....

What did I learn from this crazy experience, that I really didn't plan on doing?

Well, in the flesh—never trust Brandi when she plans a trip for her birthday! Because that girl is fearless and crazy! Lol. I love and miss her so much. And spiritually—To trust the Most High completely, no matter what. He will never leave me nor forsake me (Hebrews 13:5–6). And also, it doesn't matter how hard or how much I cry. Yahuah is not going to stop molding and shaping me because He loves me that much (John 15:2). And I also realized, once I was finished and out of the forest, how much I missed out on because of fear and lack of trust. I did not trust my guide at all. I thought he was trying to kill me, and everybody else was just blindly following him like fools. If I had just trusted my guide from the get-go and let go of my fears (allowed peace to come in) I could have really enjoyed the journey. Once we dropped off our equipment, and headed to the office to get our "I didn't die" Certificates.

There was a picture board there with all of these cool animals and sights we were supposed to have seen on the journey. The board's title was "Check off all the cool things you saw on your journey. Well, I am sure you know by now I didn't see anything—just my life flashing before my eyes. I missed out on enjoying the journey by not accepting Yahuah's peace during this process. I had to learn spiritually that it's not about hurrying up and getting through the forest. It's actually about growing and building my relationship with Yahuah while He's doing a great work in me. That's actually the best part, and I have to remind myself of that every day. So, if you are going through something right now that is making you feel like Yahuah is not there or that He doesn't love you, think again, because He is and He does. Just believe that He is closer to you than the air that you breathe. Now that's close! Because He actually is the air that you breathe!

So, you're probably asking yourself, why I am telling you this crazy story…. Well, because it rocked my soul and woke me up to helping me realize that, I can do nothing in this life without Yahuah. I was shaken for weeks after going zip lining because it literally woke up my sleeping soul that was dying.

As I look back at my zip lining experience, it has helped me to realize that, spiritually, it was the beginning of my forest season. And that was because I truly surrendered my heart to Abba, not having a clue as to what I was walking myself into. I hadn't really read the Bible or understood the journey that my ancestors had gone through because they are a stiff-necked people. So, I had no idea what I would have to go through to get to the other side, which is where I am now in 2026. I'm not going to lie, It has been a rough journey for me, only because I had to learn how to be obedient and trust Yahuah with everything. I mean everything! This woman right here had severe trust issues, due to every trauma I've been through.

Everyone in my life has let me down, I mean everyone, starting with my parents, so when Yahuah told me one day, I have to learn how to trust Him and that He is not a man and will never leave me nor forsake me, I didn't realize that I had to work through some things with him to get to that point. I now know how to let Yahuah take the wheel and have complete control. It's still not easy, and I noticed when I'm not, because I don't feel His peace. And when I don't feel His peace, I panic and I immediately ask Him, "What am I doing wrong or what did I miss?". He catches me every time. It's almost like He is spiritually clearing His throat, and I am reminded to just sit back and know that He is the Almighty (Psalms 16:10), and I can do all things through Yahusha who strengthens me (Philippians 4:13).

For the last three years, I have been in isolation and have experienced so much, including deliverance with just me and Yahuah, and even though I wouldn't want to go through any of it again, it was all worth it. I am now who He created me to be, I am a prophetic warrior for the Most High, here to help free the captives (others like me, the remnants; are those who keep Yah's Commandments and follow Him to the end). Because now, in 2026, and even when a large majority of people may be turning away from Yahuah, there is still a smaller group of faithful individuals that Yahuah is actively empowering and calling to stand strong in their faith, serving as a beacon of righteousness in a challenging time; essentially Yahuah is selecting a dedicated group to carry out His purposes, despite the surrounding negativity.

I can spiritually see myself sitting on my white horse with my full armor on, holding my bow and arrow in my hands and my quiver full of truth arrows. I have on the robe of righteousness because He put it on me after I was tested and approved by Him. Yahuah had to see that He could trust me too. He doesn't give assignments like this to just anybody. You have to be tested over and over and over again; and trust me, you can't pass any of these without the Ruach's help. I had so many deep-seated traumas all the way back to when I was five years old. He had to show them to me so that I could surrender all of it to Yahuah, and then he would heal me so that I would never have to deal with those traumas again. I had to learn how to forgive everyone who hurt me. Trust me the list is long. He took everyone from my life that I thought loved me, and He had to reveal to me that they didn't love me—not unconditionally. As long as I was being who they wanted me to be, they tolerated me. I now know what unconditional love is, so I'm careful with who I welcome into my life.

I'm telling you all of this because I wish I had someone like me to tell their story about going through the forest. Once you commit your life to Yahuah, you better hold on and never let go because you're in for a crazy ride, that will deliver and set you free. Yahusha said, I will lose not one. He left the 99 for me (Matthew 18:12, Luke 15:4) because I was heading straight to hell thinking I could do whatever I want and He would still forgive me (that's what Christianity teaches: once saved always saved—(LIES). That's the furthest from the truth. In essence, what you're doing when you're lukewarm and living your life for yourself thinking just asking for forgiveness every time will clear your name. You're actually putting Yahusha back on the stake every time. And that is not the truth. He died for you to save your soul once so you're either committed or you're not. You're either with Him or against Him there is no middle ground.

He said He will spew you out of His mouth if you are lukewarm (Revelation 3:16). He's coming back, and I believe in this generation, and he's coming back this time as the lion, for judgment. He was here before as the sacrificial Lamb and the perfect example for us to follow. But judgment is coming, and it's time to wake up and be ready for His return. Once He sees that you are serious and you want everything that Yahuah has for you, oh, you're gonna get through that forest, how long it takes depends on you. The secret sauce is obedience… when you hear His Ruach tell you to do something, do it without hesitation, no matter how crazy it looks to others. He said, "My ways are not your ways. My thoughts are not your thoughts" (Isaiah 55:8-9). So, I seek Him in everything I do, because I trust Him completely. Yahusha, when He was on this earth, was the perfect example of how we should live. Read your Bible like your life depends on it, because it does. Read it like the love story that it is from beginning to end straight through. And when you get through it, start over because the same scripture will teach you multiple things. I am convinced the Bible is alive, and it speaks to His people. You don't need anyone to teach you how to have your own relationship with your creator. Once you get on your knees, repent and ask Yahuah to fill you, He will heal, deliver and set you free and you will begin to have the best relationship you've ever experienced in your life. Just you and Abba (Father), He is all you will have and He is all that you need. How do I know this? Because I experienced it myself, and I'm still experiencing Him more and more daily. He says that He will be working on us until He returns and

I pray that He will duct tape me to His throne so that I can worship Him for all eternity. That is my true heart's desire, and He knows it.

I am excited about zip lining again one day, being the new me, just to see how it will be. This is because I embarrassed myself the last time. I might even go back and look for the same tour guide so that I can show him the new me and hand him my book. I can do all things through Yahusha, who strengthens me (Philippians 4:13).

So, after my Zip lining experience, it has been an interesting and challenging thing to completely give all control to Yahuah. But I knew that that is what I had to do. Zip lining showed me who I was at the time and how much work needed to be done to get me to who I am today. It was a long, hard journey, and it's still challenging, but as I do my five steps more and more each day, this journey is worth it. When I start to slip and try to take the reins, I hear the ever-patient Ruach reminding me to trust Him. You see, my natural fleshly reaction is to take the wheel. But my heart knows that Yahuah is much better at it than I am. So, I fight to let go and allow Abba to have complete control. My life has been so much better this way. As I look back at all the things I have been through in my life, some with Abba and some trying to handle them on my own, I come to a very clear understanding: Life has its ups and downs, and having the almighty Yahuah cradling you in His hands during your process is the best place to be. I feel like I'm just floating on water. It's so much easier this way. Before, I felt like I was doggy paddling with my head barely above the water, waiting on Yahuah to save me. When Yah told me to just let go, and just relax, and trust Him all the craziness stopped. I just had to obey. Mind you, He was telling me this all along—I was being disobedient. I'm going to leave you with this last thought:......don't you want to know why you're here?

Don't you want to know why Yahuah created you? Don't you want a real relationship with your Creator? Stop chasing what the world has to offer (which is temporary gratification), and become who He created you to be. You can only do that when you allow Yahuah to fill you completely.

I don't mean just give Him a little space, like when you go to church on Sunday. These churches are deceiving; they give you a false sense of peace. The real peace only comes from Yah, and you only get that when you're walking in obedience—when you have surrendered everything to him

PLEASE get on your knees and repent, for we are all sinners; we all fall short of His glory (Romans 3:23). Ask our Creator to forgive you and then ask Him to fill you with His spirit (Ruach ha Kodesh), so He can set you free, so, you can be who He created you to be. When He sees that you're serious, He will come in and do a great work in you. Then, spend time with Him daily, so that He can show you who He is, and by doing that you will learn who you are in Him, and I promise your life will change forever. For the better. Last, but very important: Once you have repented and asked Yahuah to fill you with His Ruach. Don't forget to do the 5 things I told you about earlier in the book. It's the 5 things He taught me to do. And I'm going to share them with you again! Now, if you work on these 5 things daily, I can promise you, you will have a real relationship with Yahuah, your creator:

1. Pray everyday and often
2. Abide: Just sit and listen for Yahuah to respond. He loves when you are focused on only Him, even if it's for 10 minutes.
3. Worship daily. It keeps the enemy away and it gives Yahuah glory.
4. Read your Bible! Start in Genesis and just read all the way through like the love story it is. Get the hidden books. You can get the Cepher and they are all there in order. This will show Yahuah you really want to get to know Him and obey His laws.
5. Fast!! Fasting helps you die to your flesh so that you can hear him better. And it's so good for you mentally and physically, I know it's not easy but its so worth it. If you do these 5 things, you will never be the same. Then all you have to focus on is obeying. Halleluiah! You can thank me later. Baruch!

Glossary:

Yahuah: Our Creator and creator of all things for His good.

Yahusha: Yahuah's only begotten Son and Yahuah's word (John 1:14).

Ruach ha Kodesh: Yahuah's spirit often depicted as a "wind" or "breath" that empowers, guides, and brings spiritual insight to individuals, enabling prophecy or extraordinary capabilities.

Die to self: Meaning surrendering everything, all idols that come before Yahuah, surrendering them to Him and keeping Yahuah first in all things. Dying to self simply means not allowing your fleshly desires to rule your life

Stiff-necked people: a people that are disobedient and refuse to obey Yahuah's laws and covenants.

Obedience: to Yahuah shows Him that you love Him. But also includes understanding that He wants you to just be His daughter/son.

Mastema- Satan, Baal, Lucifer, or Buddha. He has many names like God, Lord, and Jesus Christ. He is the enemy of our souls. His goal in life is to take as many, of Yahuah's precious humans to hell with him as possible, proving that humanity is rotten. He wants to prove to Yahuah that He should have never created us. He hates humanity that much.

Holy Spirit: The term "Holy Spirit" originates from a combination of Hebrew and Greek biblical, linguistic, and theological roots. It stems from the Hebrew Ruach ha-Kodesh (divine breath/wind) in the Old Testament, which was translated into Greek as Pneuma

Hagion in the New Testament and later to Latin as Spiritus Sanctus, describing the third person of the Trinity

"Holy Ghost" vs. "Holy Spirit": "Holy Ghost" was the traditional English translation from Old English gast (meaning soul, breath, spirit), popular in the 1611 King James Bible. Over the 20th century, this shifted to "Holy Spirit" as "ghost" developed connotations of a specter or, in modern terms, a dead person's spirit.

Where did the name "Holy Spirit" come from?

Christianity. For the large majority of Christians, the Holy Spirit (or Holy Ghost, from Old English gast, "spirit") is the third person of the Trinity: the "Triune God" manifested as Father, Son, and Holy Spirit; each Person being God. *In my humble opinion, it's pagan because it came from England. It had nothing to do with Hebrew or Yahuah.*